Be Seeded: Collages Made from a Single Photograph by Bree

Least Bittern Books
Henry County, KY

Least Bittern Books
147 Marcus St. #4
Pleasureville, KY
40057

In$ults & Inquiries
please send commissions or
order prints/canvas reproductions
of Bree's collage or drawings to
greenpandapress@gmail.com

find more work by this artist at
theartistbree.com and Facebook

copywhat 2017

Be Seeded is my selection of Buddhist-inspired collages made from a single photograph. Whether i see a bodhisattva in the paths worms made in a sitting log or all of the female energy among the outer-workings of a tractor, i use the program Paint to cut and paste from a photograph until my figure emerges in-full. i use Fotor, Photos or Adobe Photoshop Express to enhance a collage. Seeing orifices where orifices ain't is my lot; mindfulness which is mine when i want it enables me as an artist to do well of must.

xoxo Bree

Need Not

I wanted something, but it was the
World, not me, who knew just what
That something was.

I found something inside me I was
The only one in the world to ever find.
It turned out to be everything in the
World I would ever need,
Instructions included:

    Need not, for what you should discover
    In any person, whosoever, on the road
    That winds back and fore, through all
    Eternity is also thine

Wood Buddha 2.23.17 Collage made from a single photograph of chopped wood in Waddy, KY made on Paint.

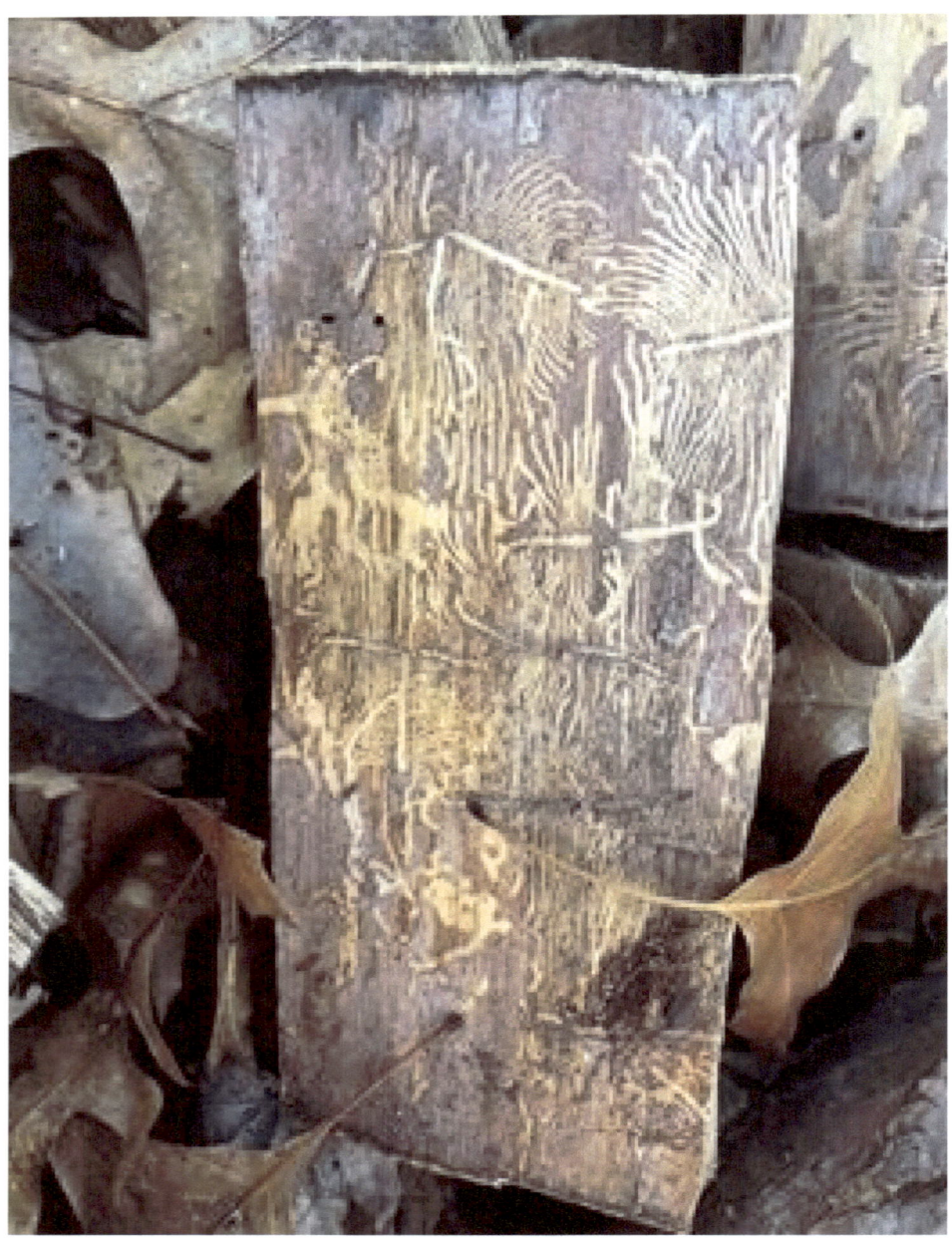

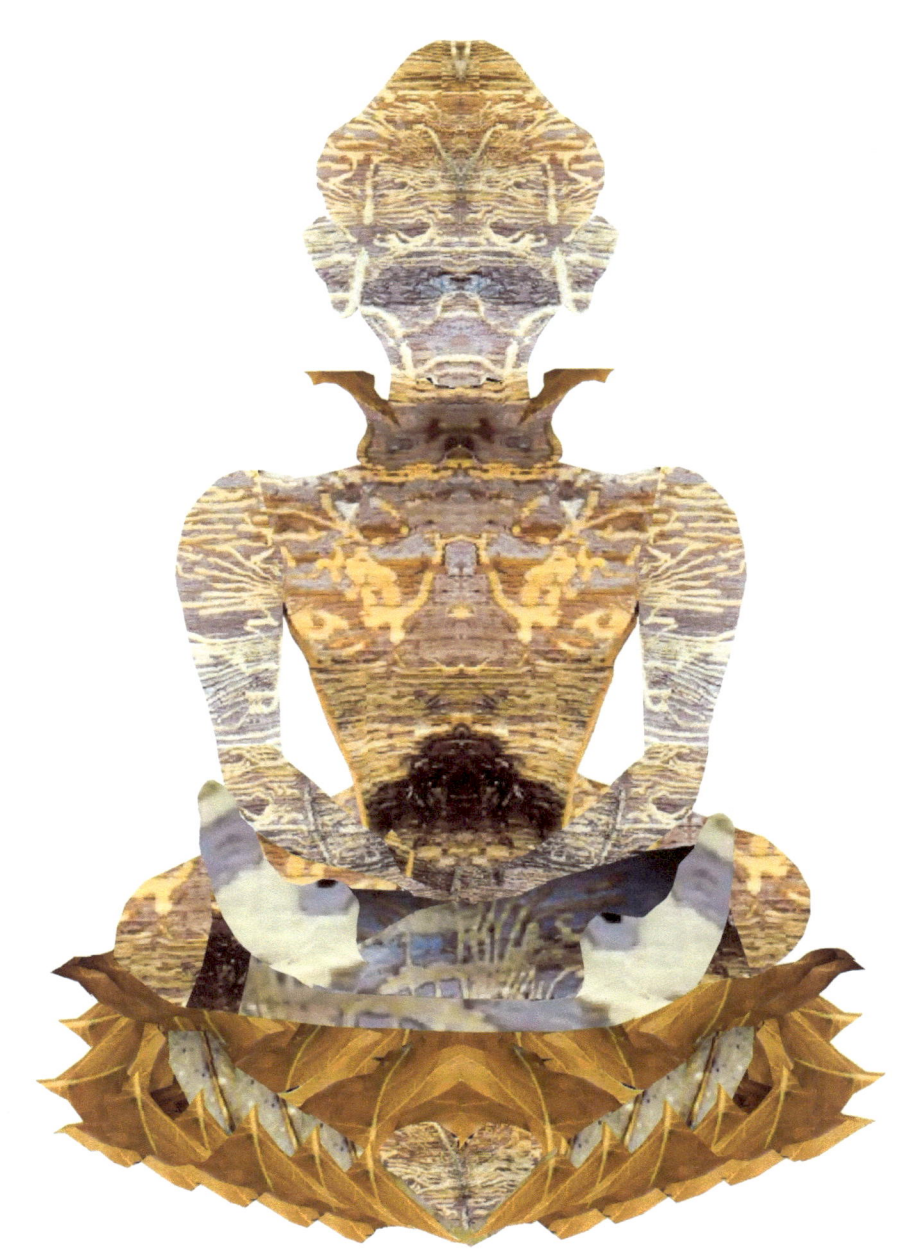

4 Wheel Bodhi 2.4.17 Collage made from a single photograph of a truck in Waddy, KY made on Paint, enhanced with Adobe Photoshop Express.

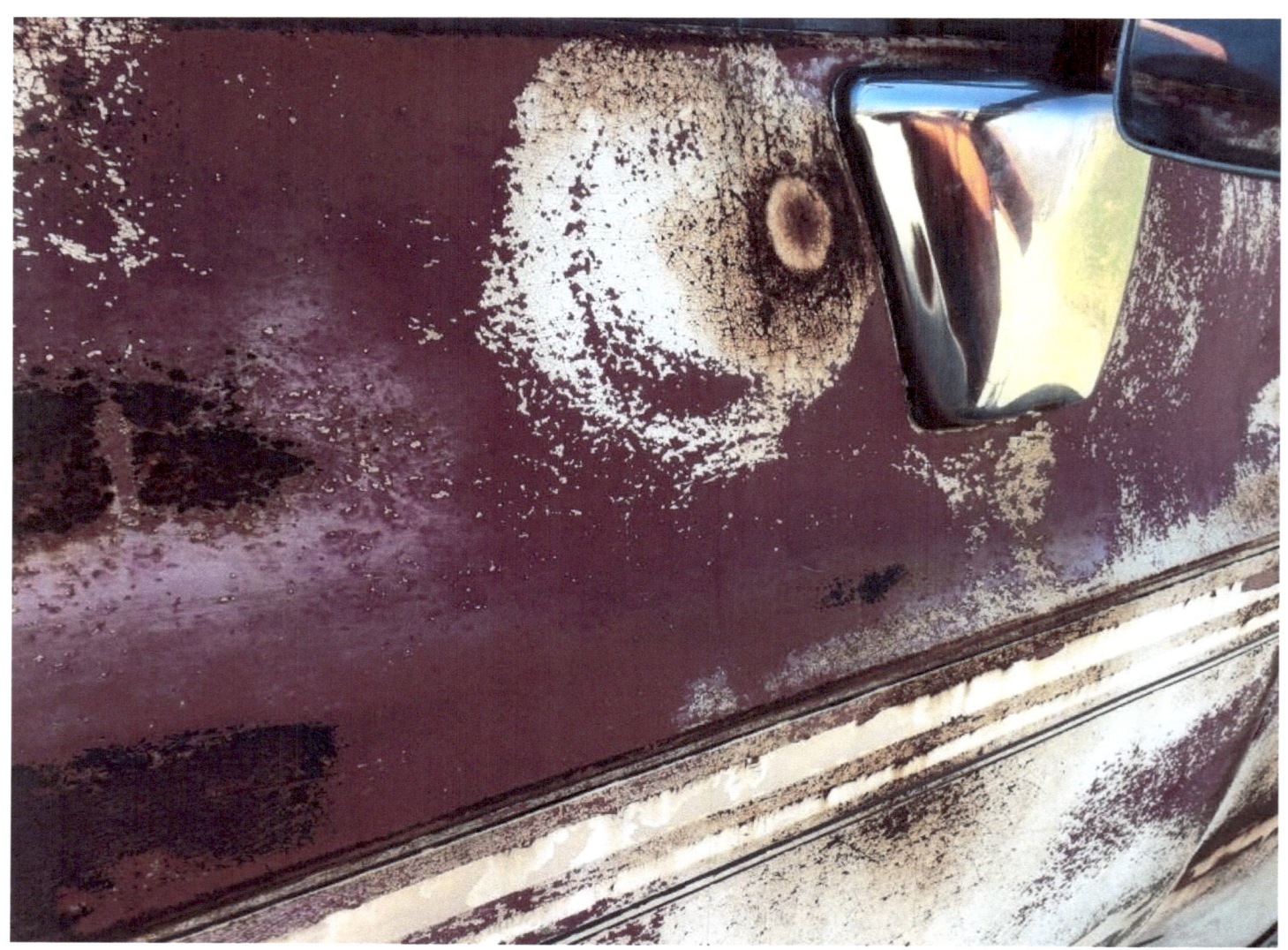

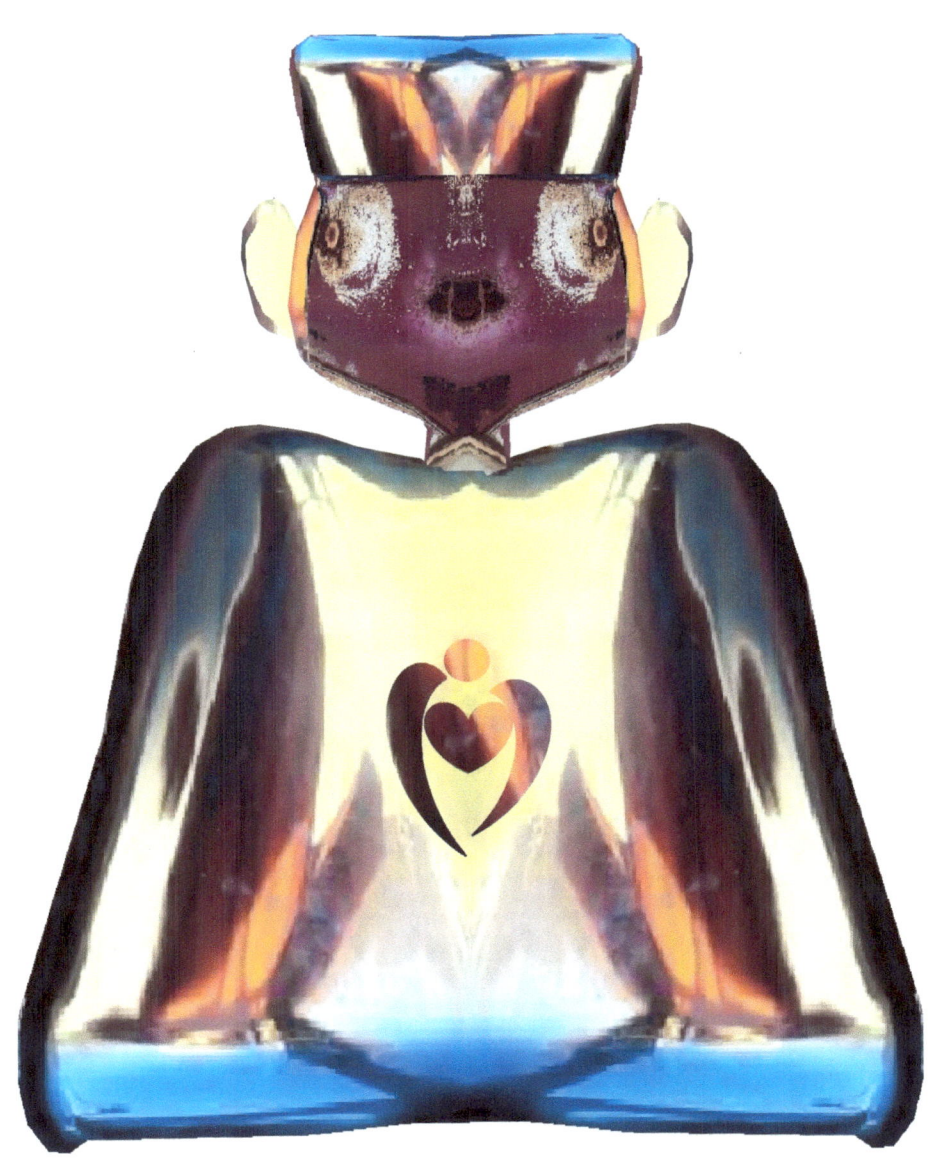

Guanyin Buddha of Compassion Goddess of Mercy 6.13.17 Collage made from a single photograph of a dog's water dish taken in Waddy, KY made on Paint, enhanced with Adobe Photoshop Express.

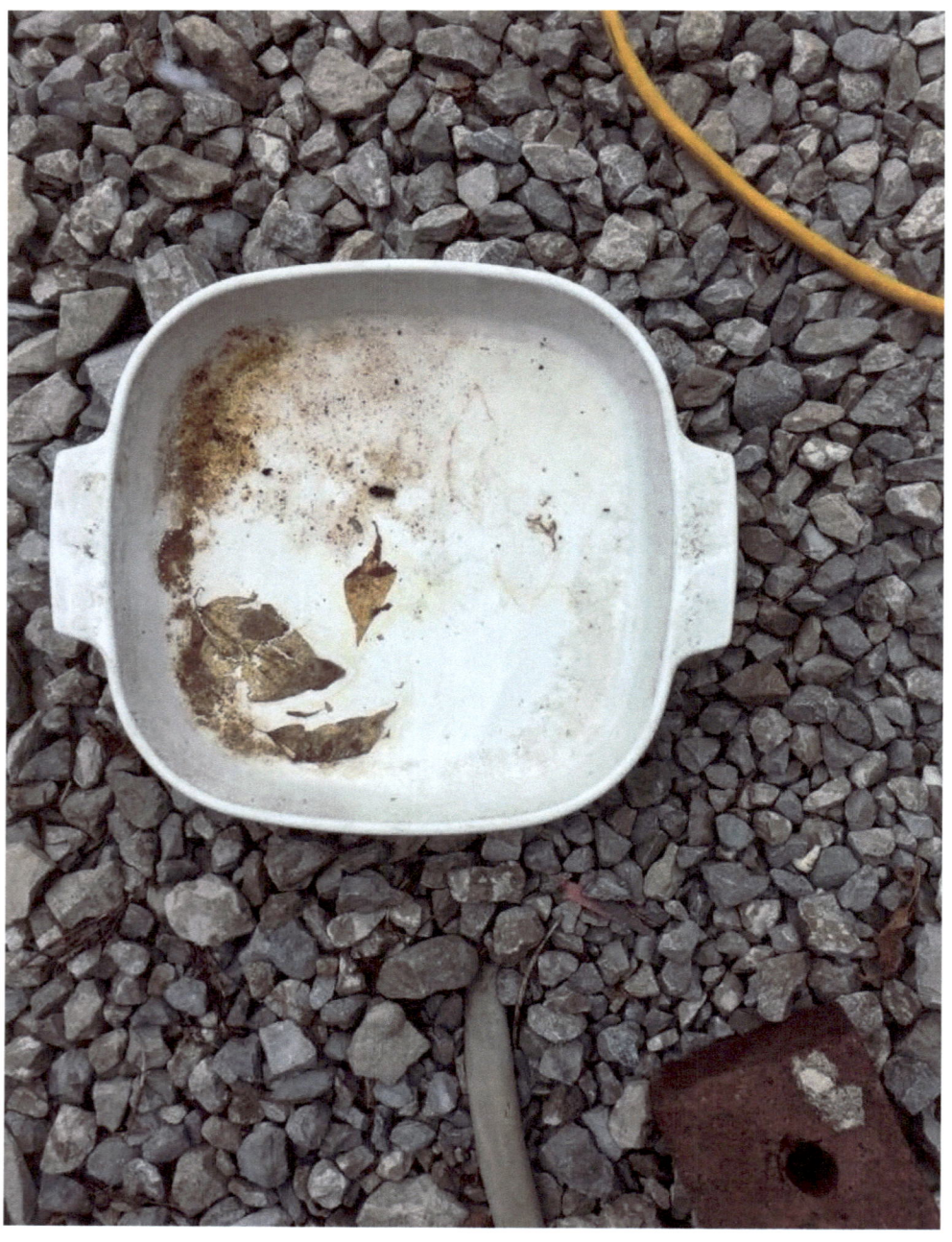

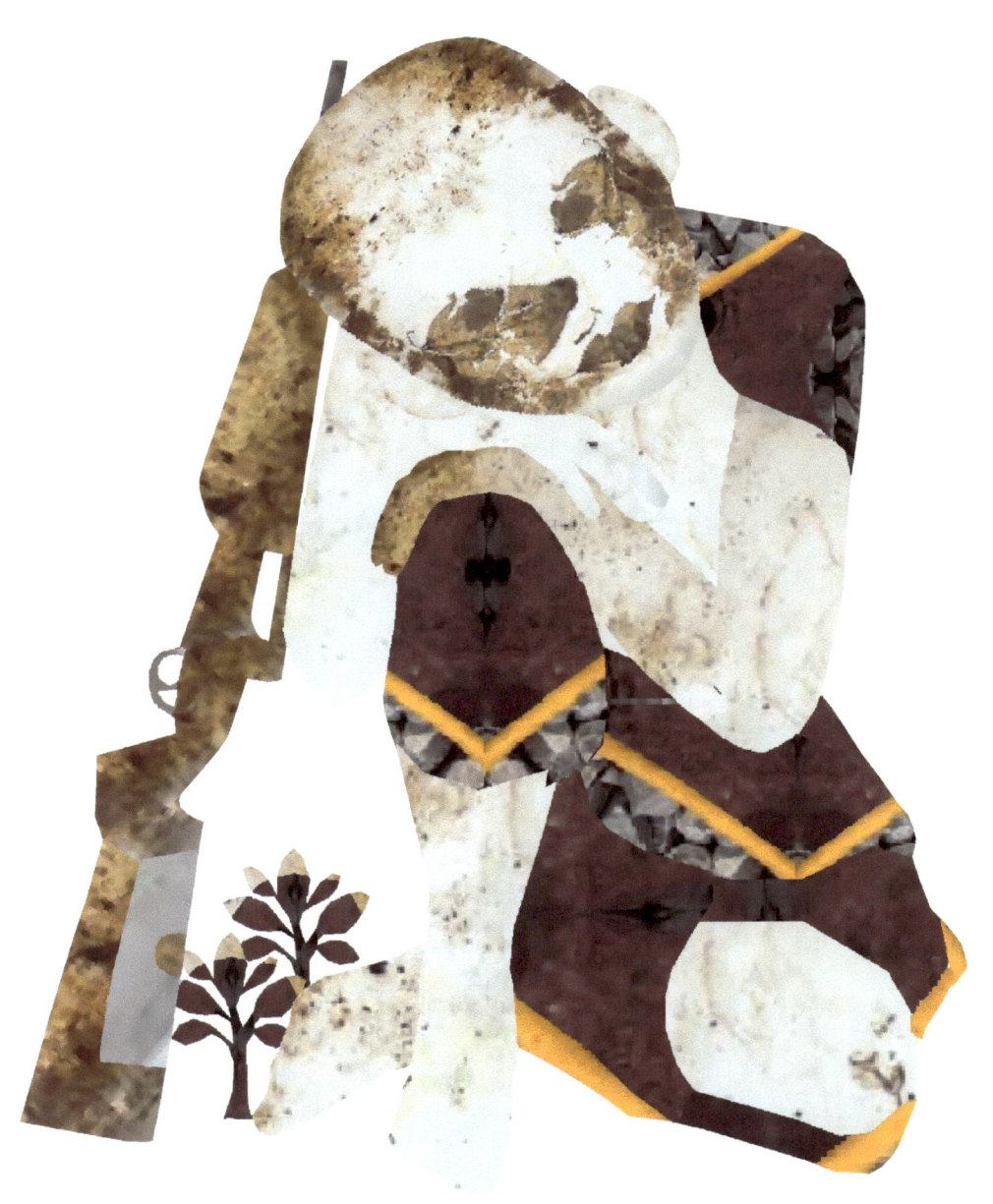

Bodhi of the Clouds 12.3.17 Collage made from a single photograph taken in Waddy, KY made on Paint, enhanced with Adobe Photoshop Express..

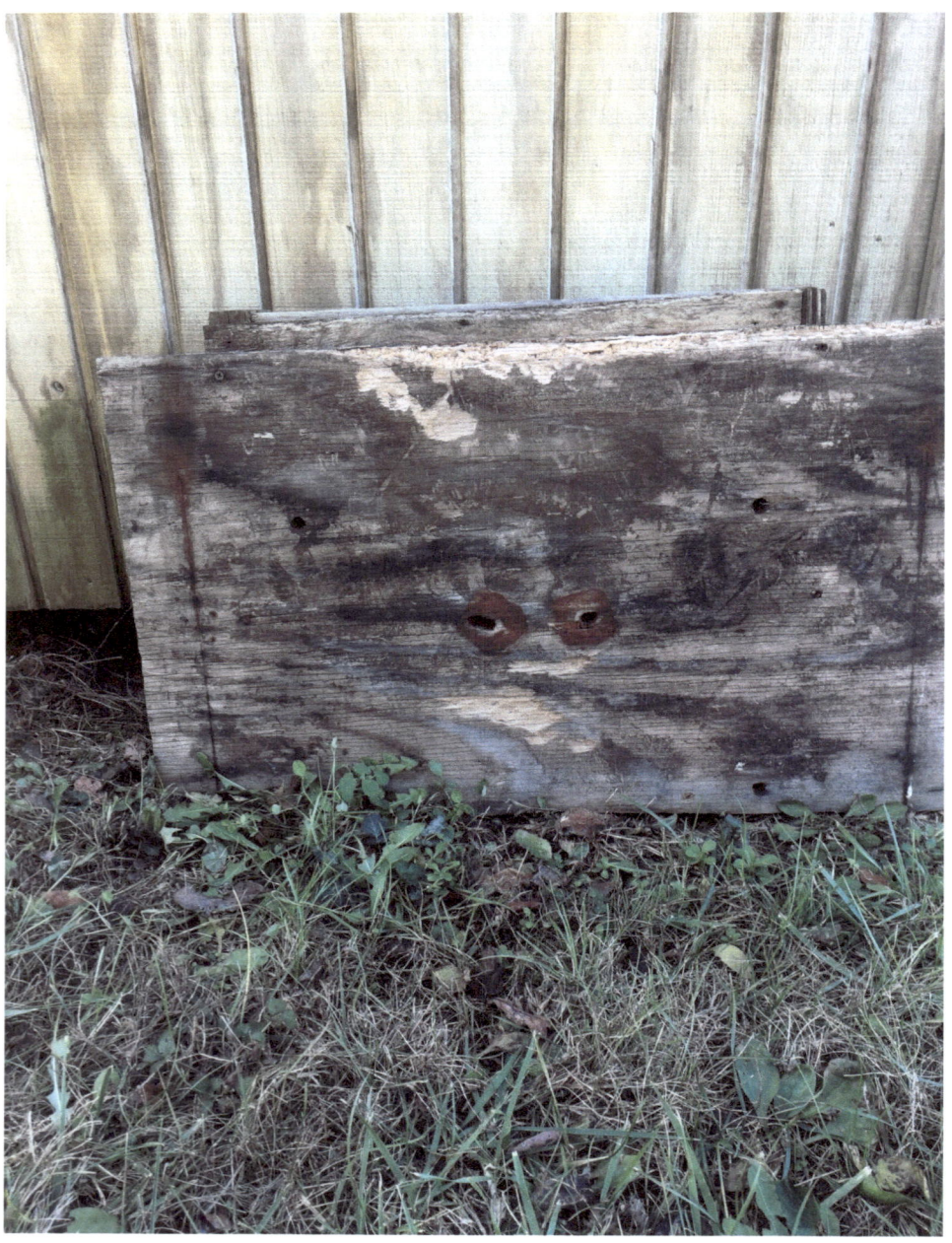

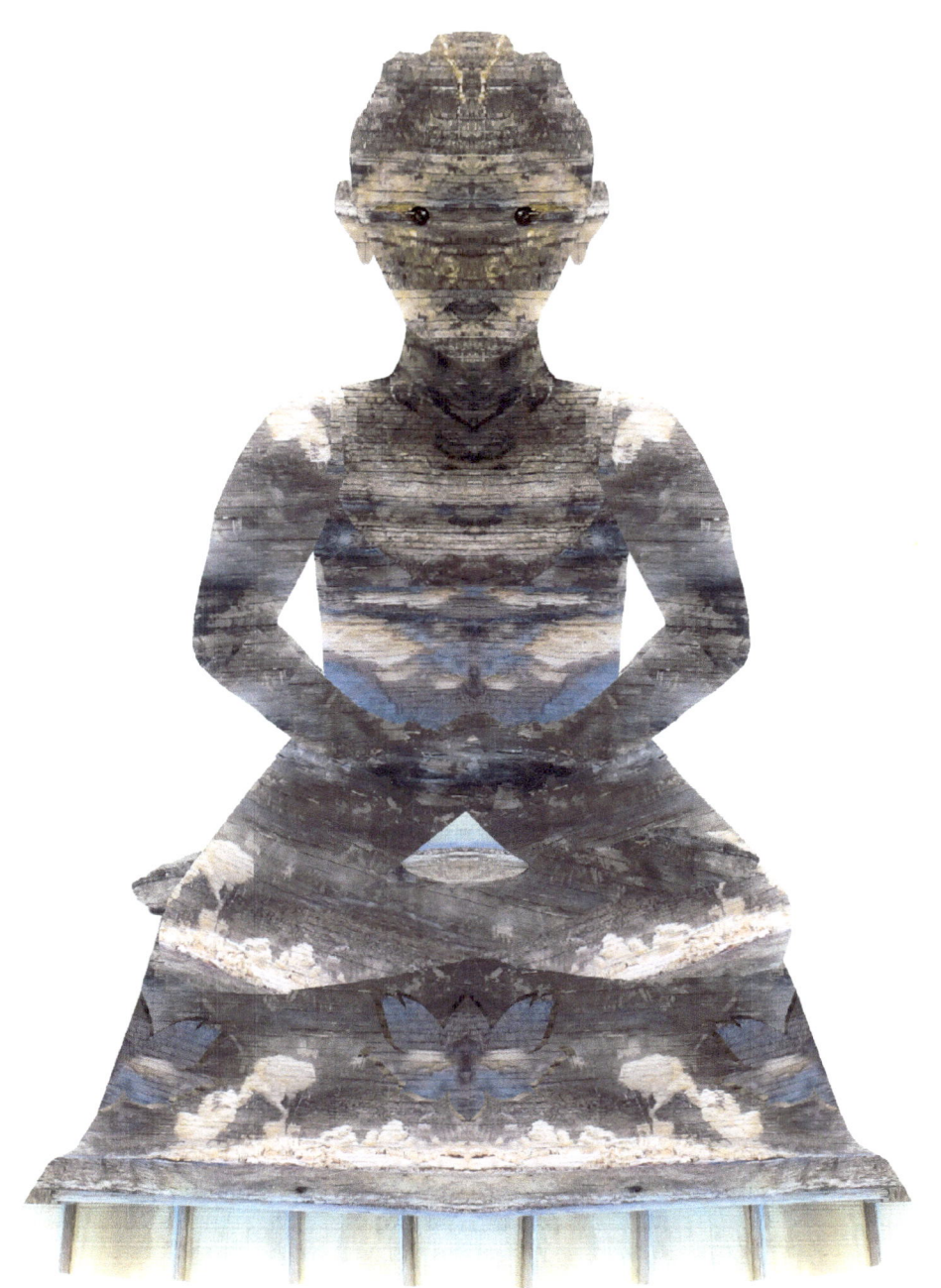

Self-Protection 5.27.17 Collage made from a single photograph of a tire taken in Waddy, KY made on Paint, enhanced with Adobe Photoshop Express.

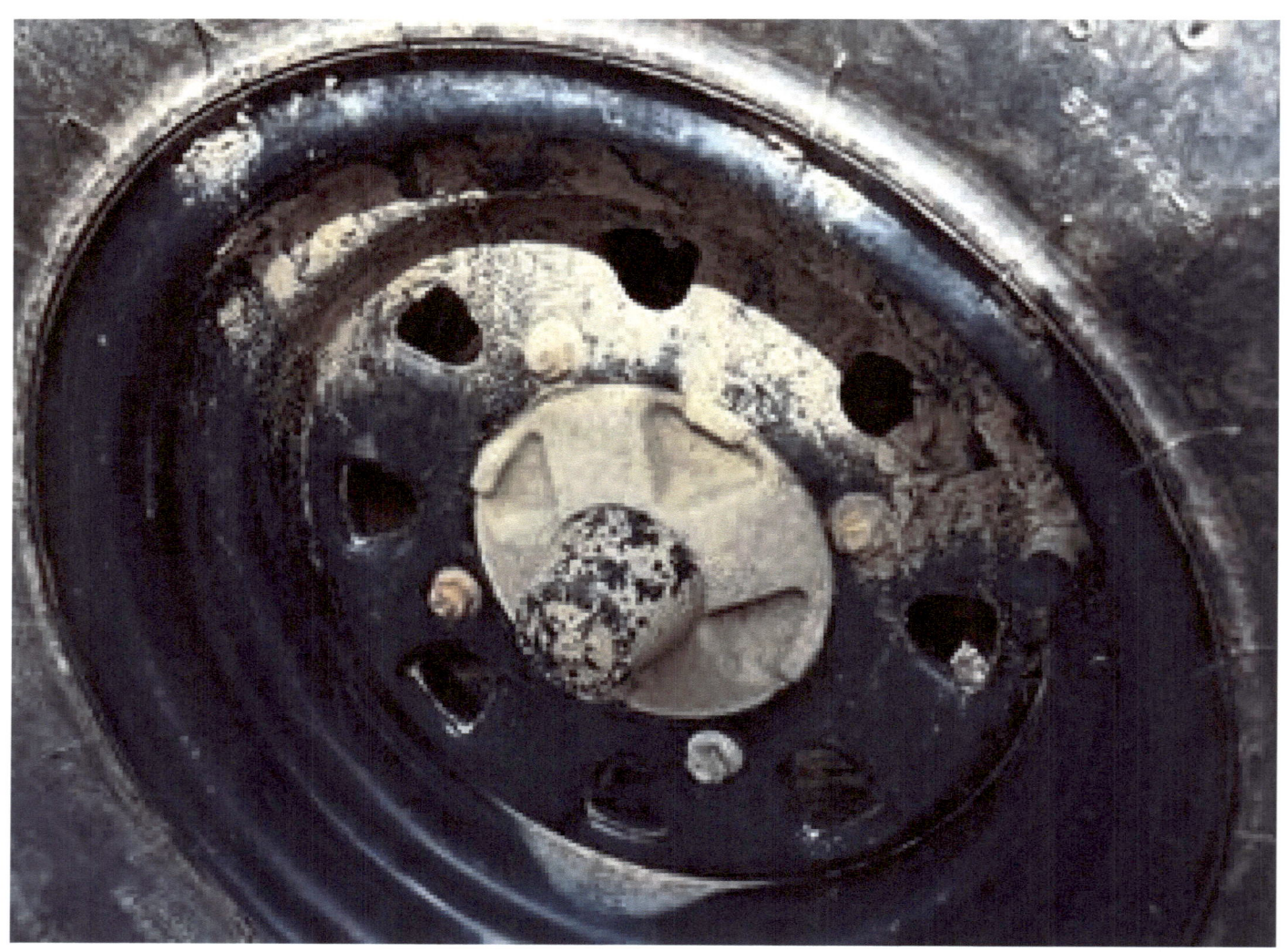

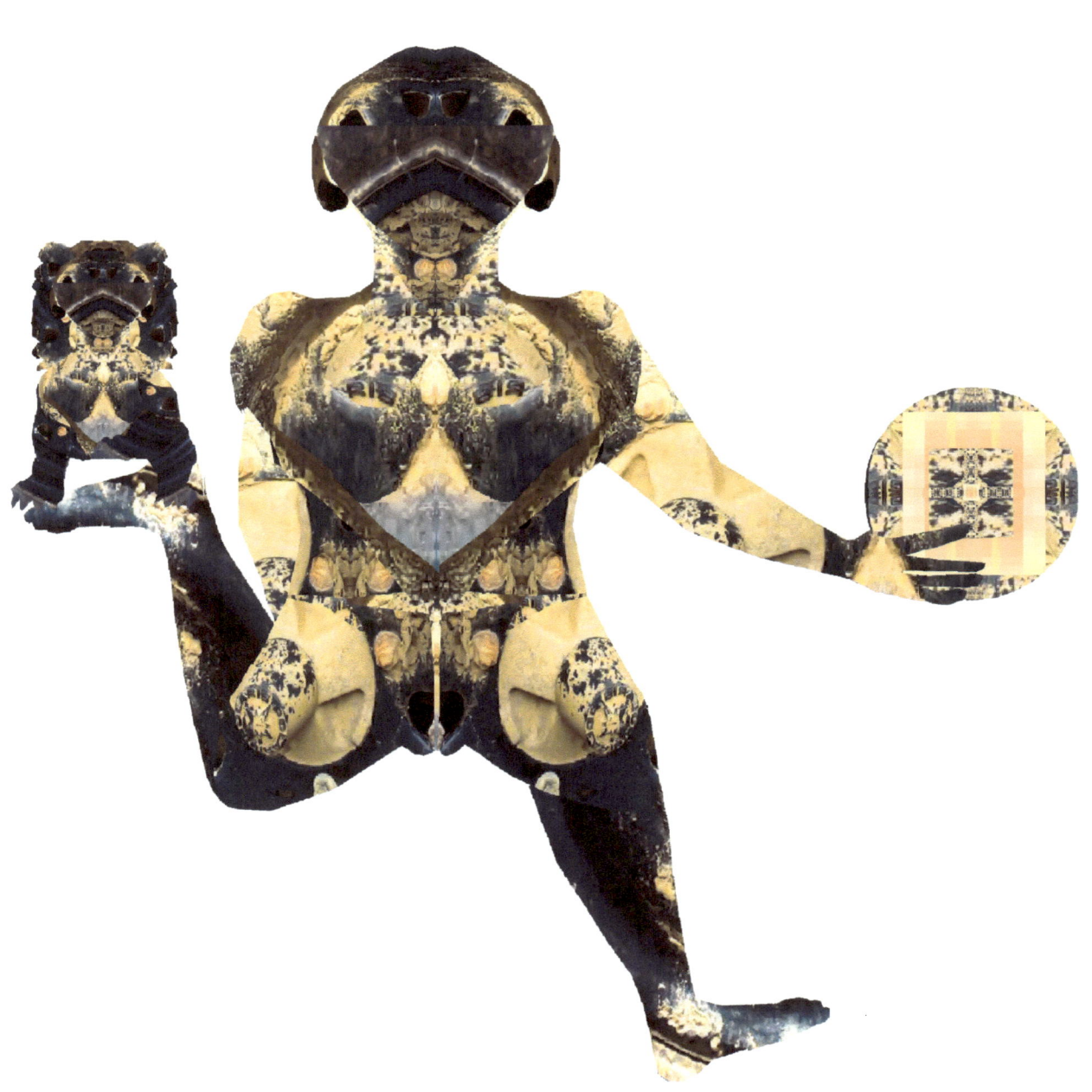

Yogi 1.9.17 Collage made from a single photograph of a door hinge in Pleasureville, KY made on Paint, enhanced with Fotor..

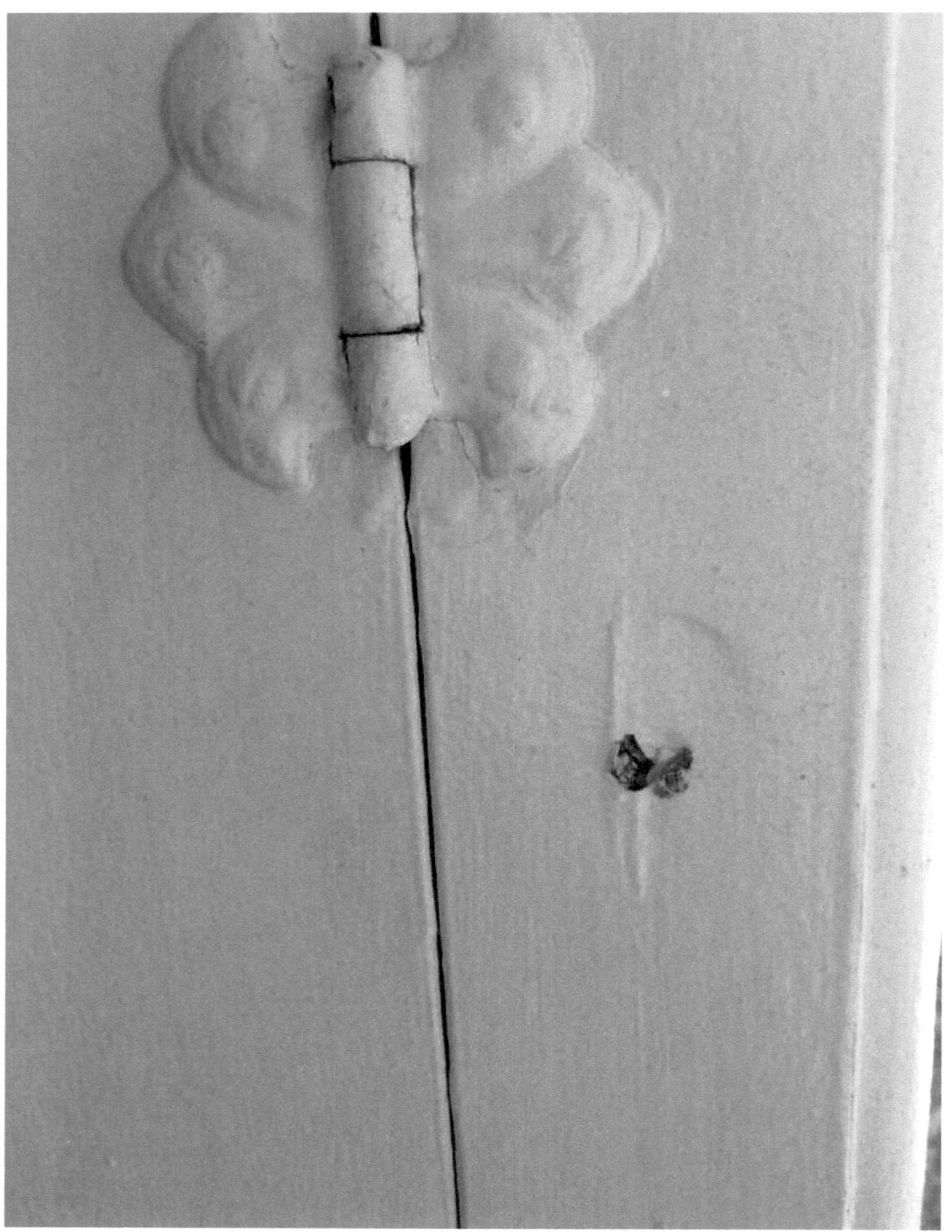

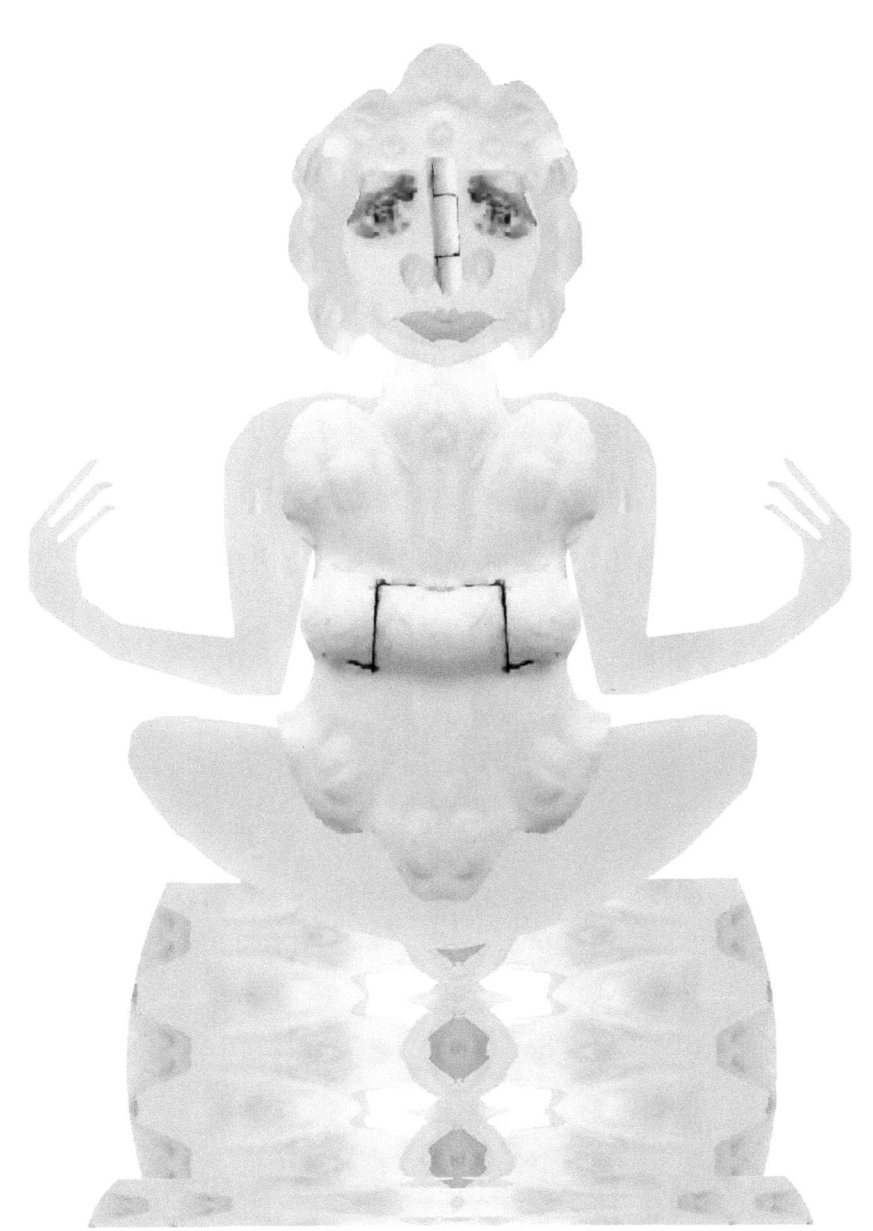

Bodhisattva of the Fox 12.18.19 Collage made from a single photograph of a tree in Oldham County, KY made on Paint, enhanced with Fotor..

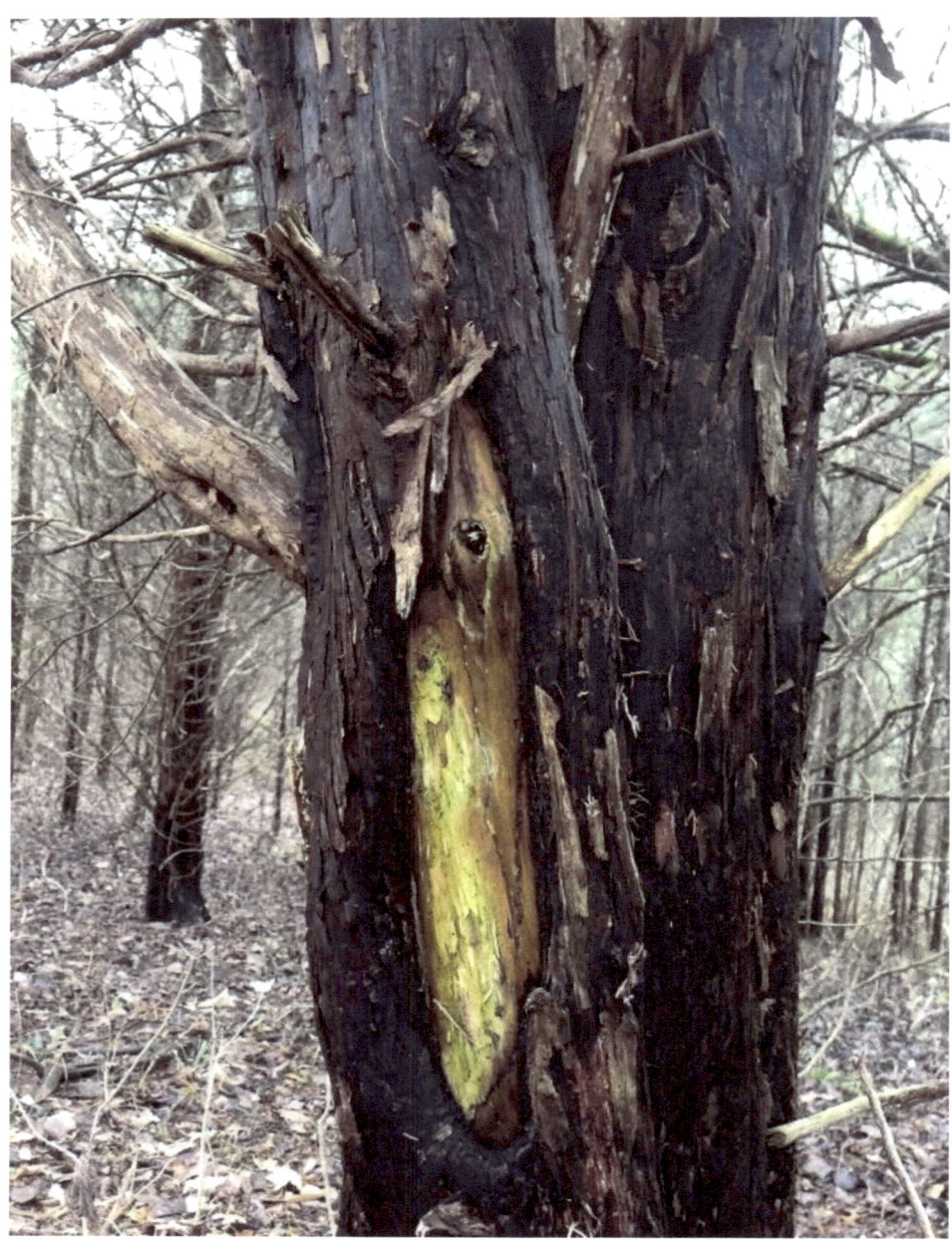

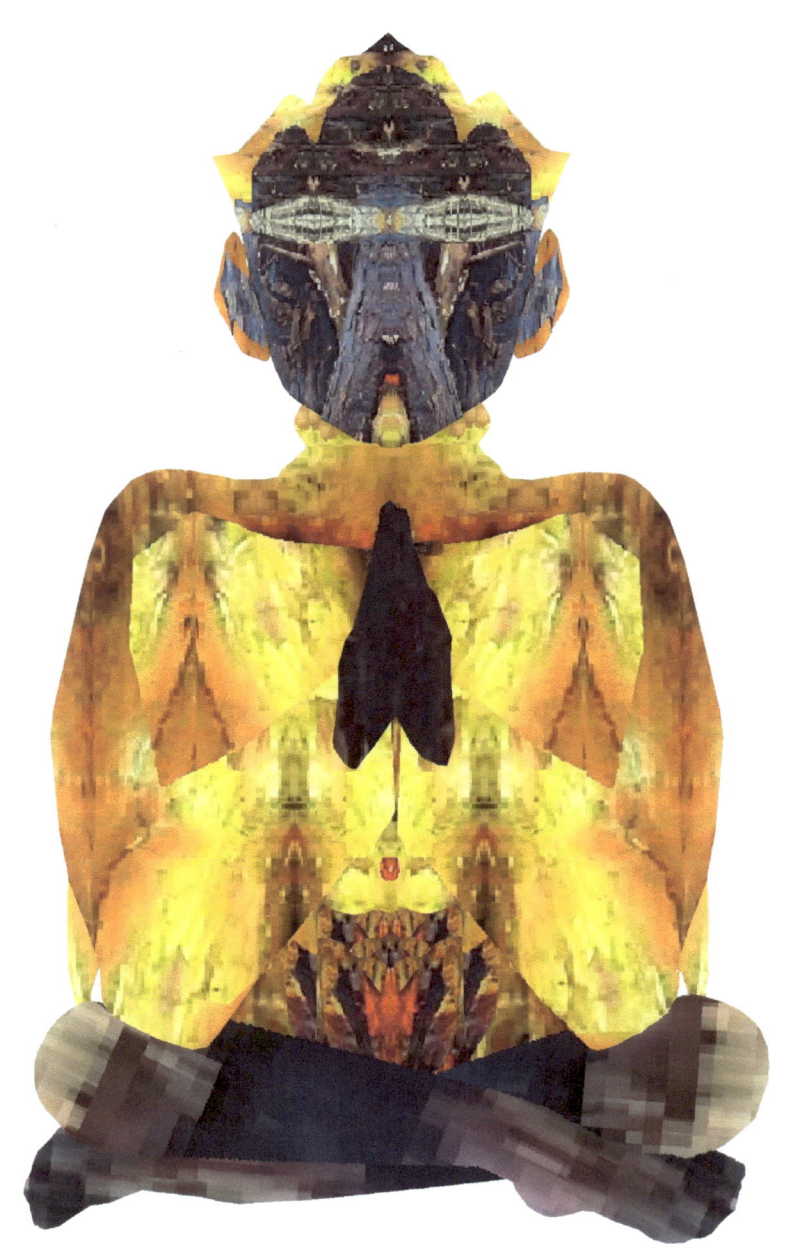

Shakti 11.19.17 Collage made from a single photograph of a tractor in Waddy, KY made on Paint, enhanced with Fotor.

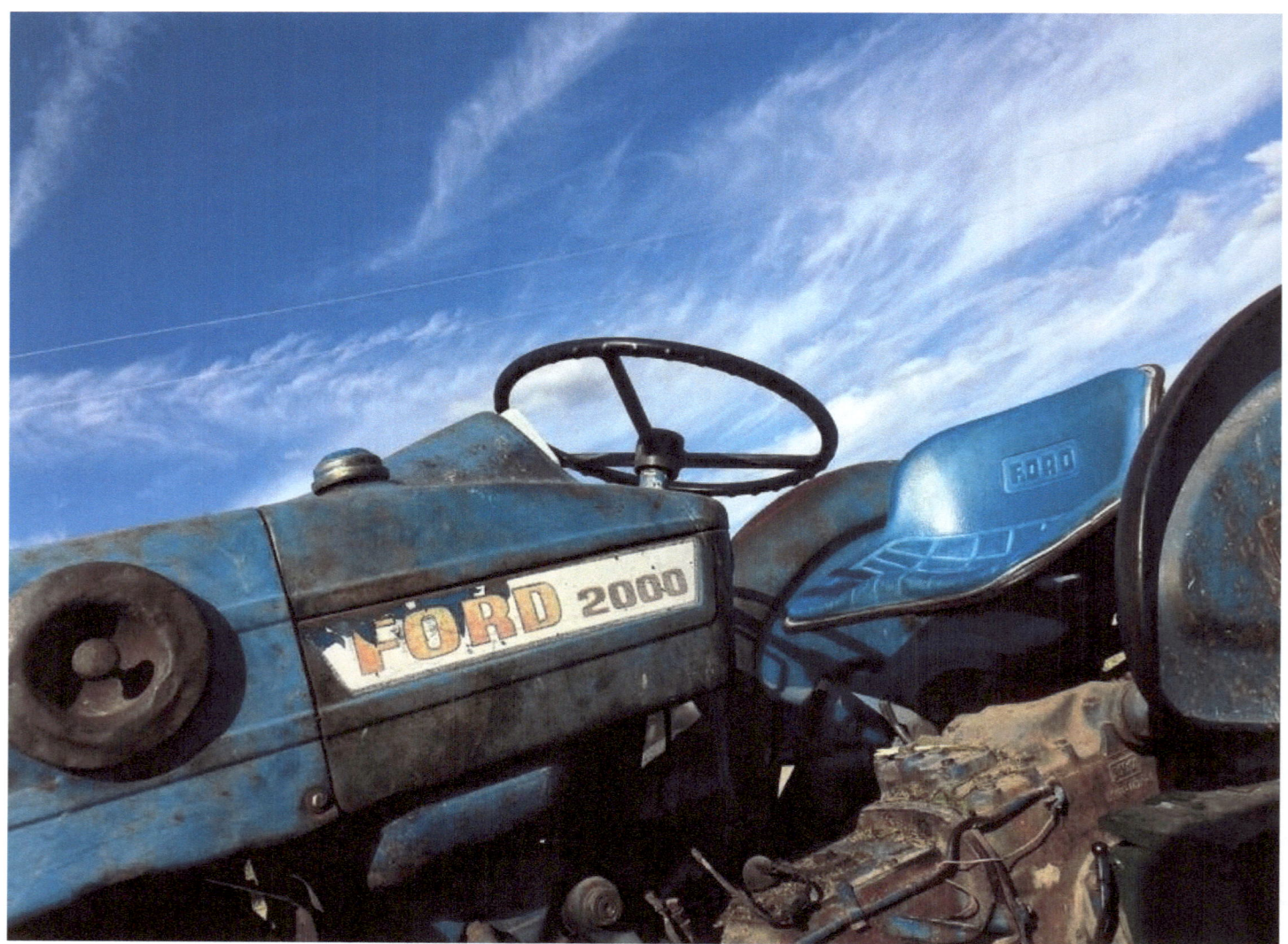

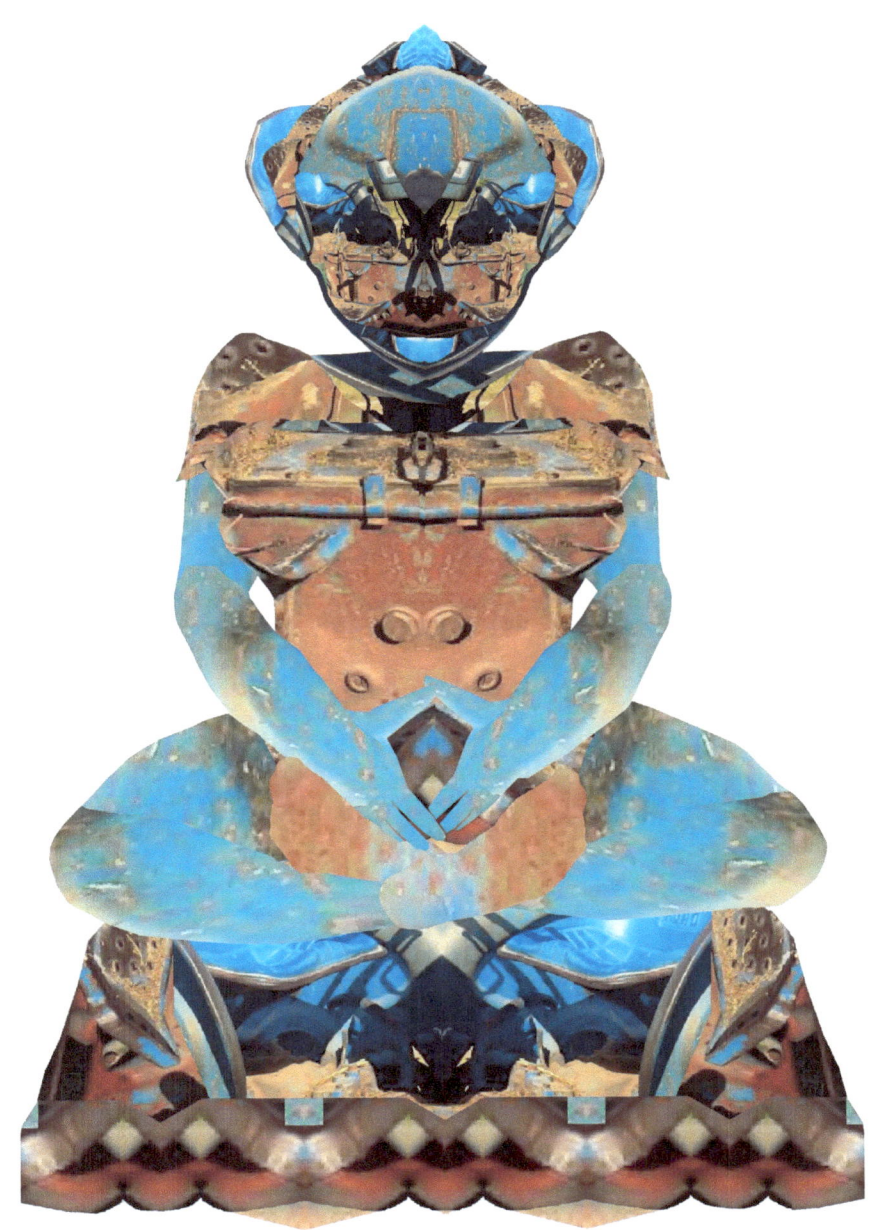

Ohm 10.26.17 Collage made from a single photograph of a bud in Mt. Eden, KY made on Paint, enhanced with Fotor..

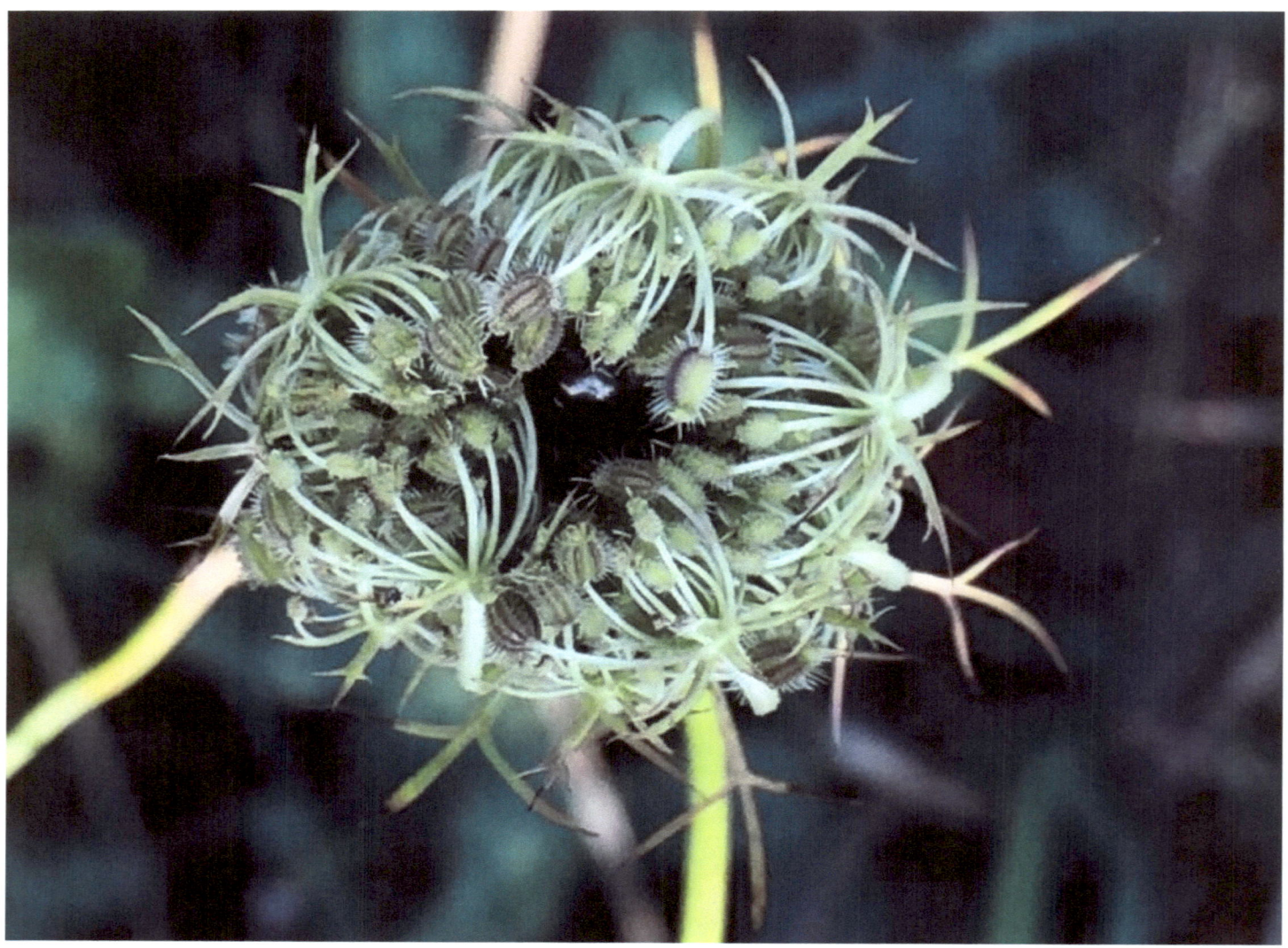

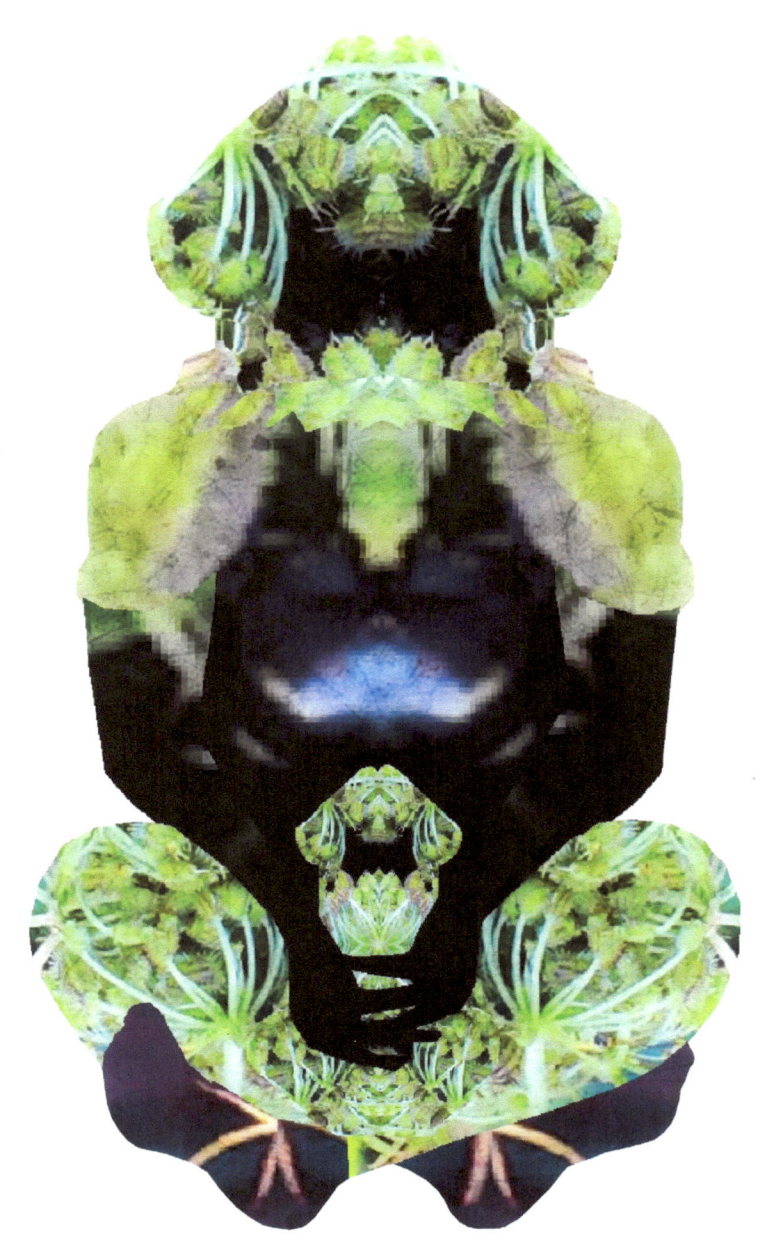

Siddhartha 5.20.17 Collage made from a single photograph of a a building exterior taken in Shelbyville, KY made on Paint, enhanced with Adobe Photoshop Express.

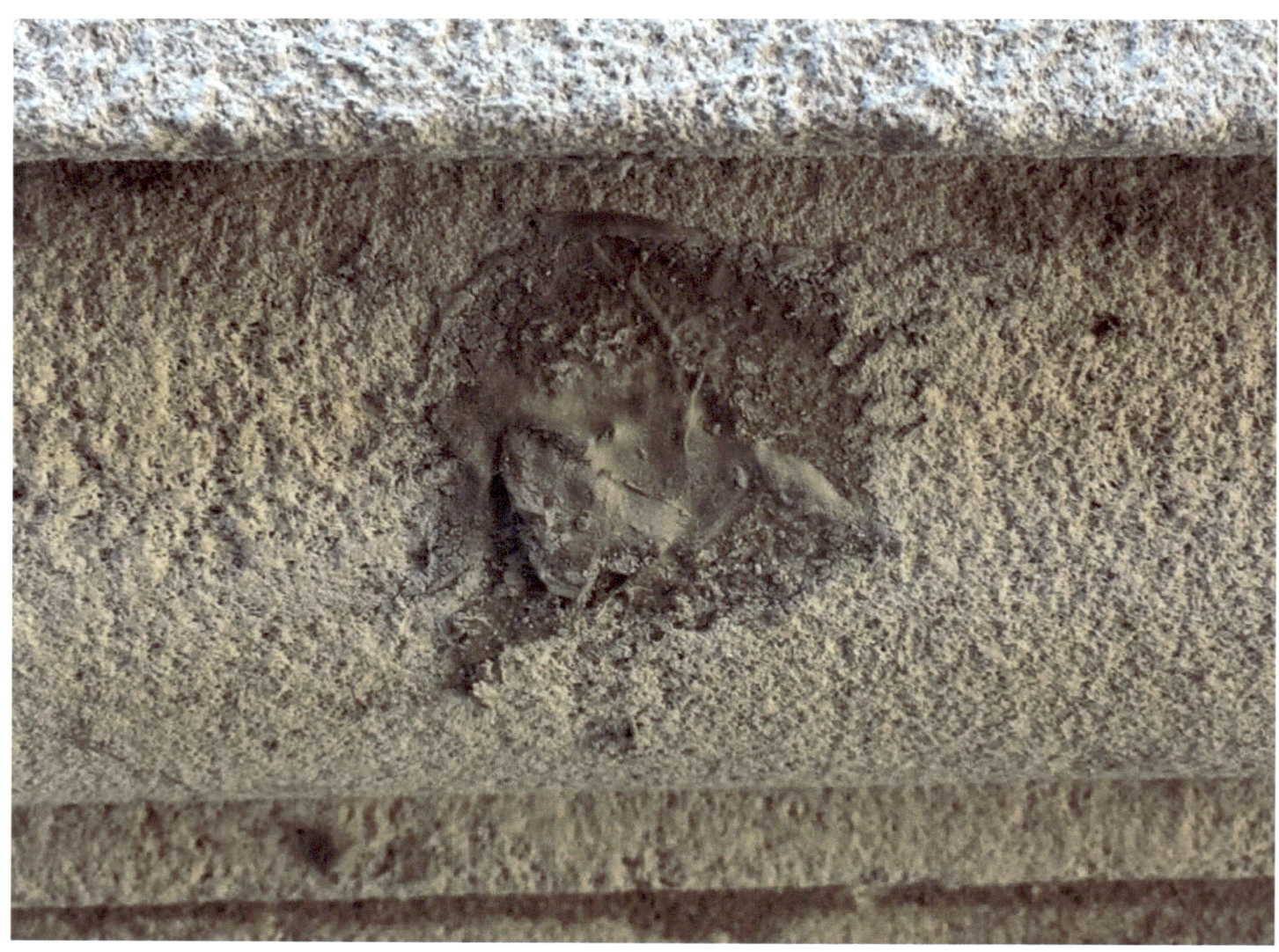

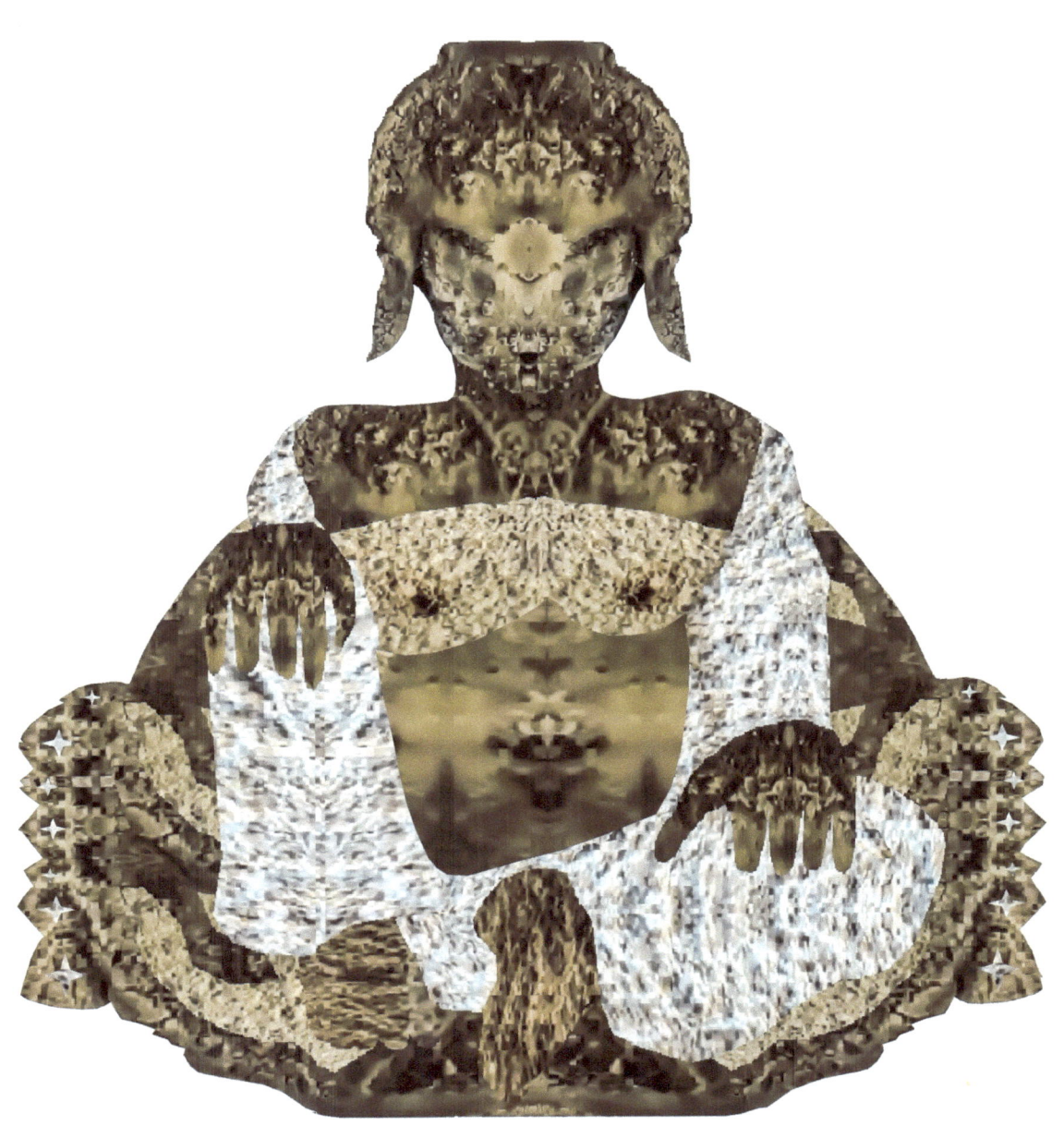

Space Buddha 12.31.16 Collage made from a single photograph of me standing near General Sherman in the Redwood Forest made on Paint, enhanced with Fotor and Photos.

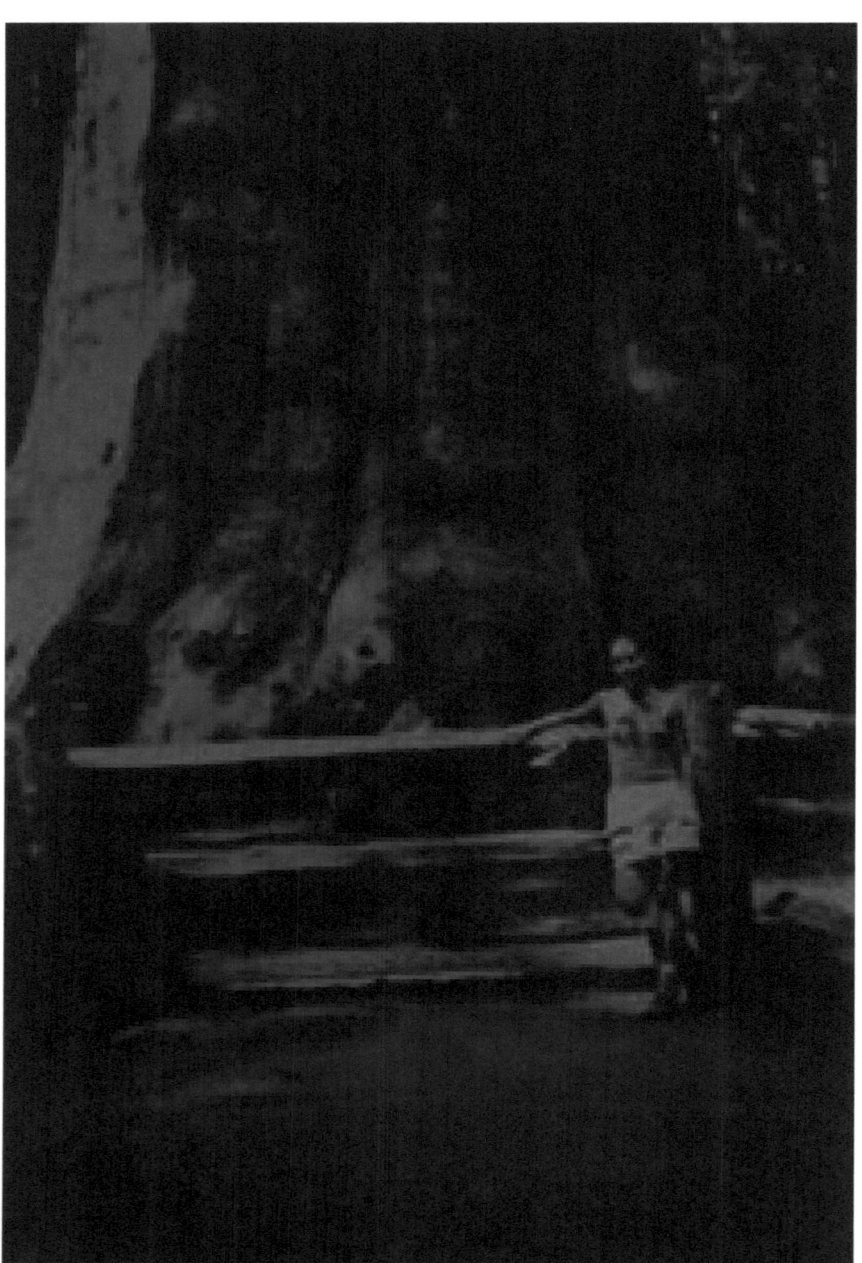

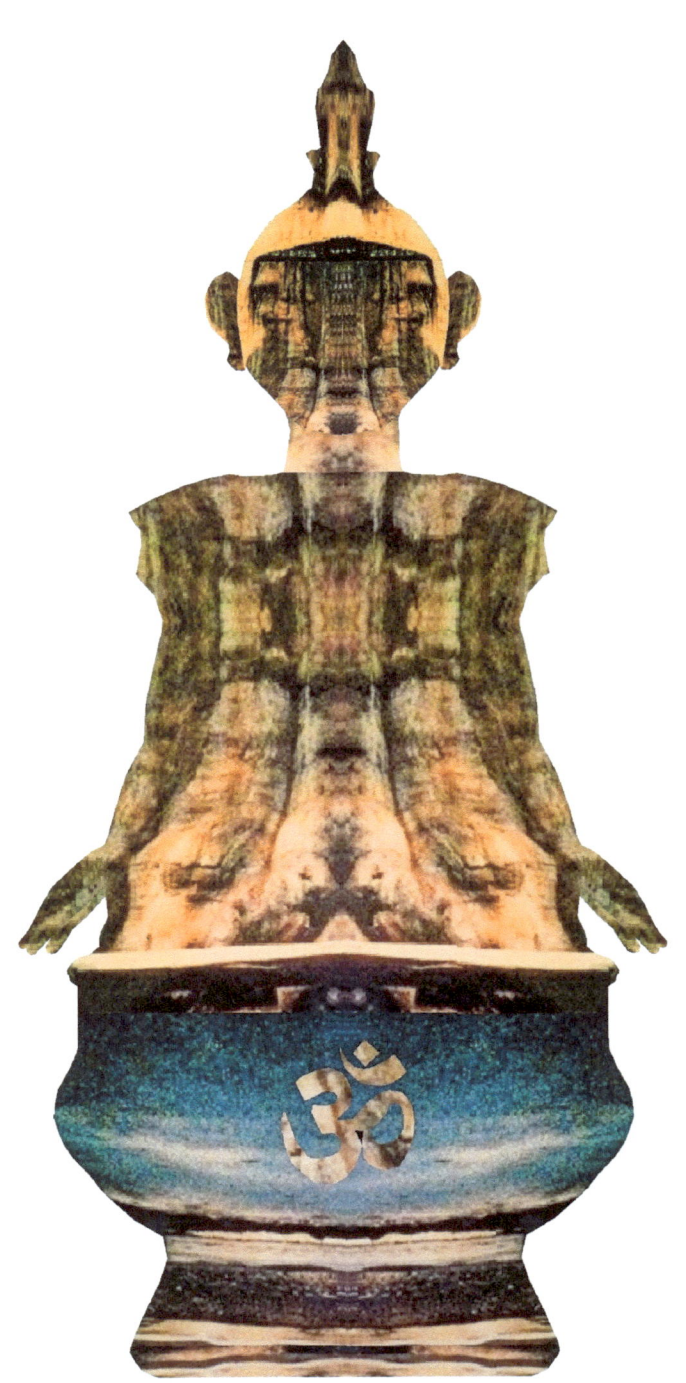

*And we all know the way
and we all see at times
yet some walk the beam
while others must strive.
And yet in colliding we
tend to remind one another
to lay low, to hover and let it all go -
 and to live without knowing the way.*

*And there isnt any age when life eases
up cus its all the same, we're just different.
And the leaf speaks the same as poet or
philosopher – knowing what's what
takes homogenous thought and a
rhythm-trained ear, for progress
travels in sound aging want for the
music life lends to the listening*

    -Bree